GATEWAYS

Morning
Evening
Birthdays
Fairytales

A collection of
Poems, Songs and Stories
for young children

Wynstones
Press

Published by
Wynstones Press
Ruskin Glass Centre
Wollaston Road
Stourbridge
West Midlands DY8 4HE.
England.
Telephone: +44 (0) 1384 399455
Email: info@wynstonespress.com

First Published 1978 by Wynstones Press
Second edition with music 1983
Fully revised third edition 1999. Reprinted 2005.

Editors: Jennifer Aulie and Margret Meyerkort

Cover and text illustrations by David Newbatt

Typeset by Wynstones Press.
Printed in the EU by Cambrian Printers.

British Library CIP data available.

ISBN 0 946206 51 1

Gateways

This is one in a series of 6 books:
Spring, Summer, Autumn, Winter, Spindrift and Gateways.

The four seasonal books comprise a wide selection of poems, songs and stories appropriate to the time of year, including much material for the celebration of festivals.

Spindrift contains verses and songs describing the world of daily work and practical life, together with a selection of stories from around the world.

Gateways comprises verses and songs for the Morning time, the Evening time and to accompany a variety of traditional Fairytales, together with poems, songs and stories for the celebration of Birthdays.

Warmest thanks to all who have contributed to and supported this work: parents, teachers and friends from Steiner Waldorf Schools in Australia, Britain, Canada, Eire, Estonia, New Zealand, Norway, South Africa and the United States. Grateful thanks also to publishers who have permitted the use of copyright material, acknowledgements for which are at the end of the volume.

INDEX

The Value of Music in the Life of the Young Child . . . 9

Recommended Reading 94

Indexes of first lines

MORNING POEMS

Awake, the sun is shining bright 20

Cock-a-doodle-doo gets up with the sun 21

Down is the earth 20

Early in the morning 22

Good morning, dear earth 18

Oh sun, so bright 19

Take my brush, take my broom 24

The golden sun is shining 23

The moon on the one hand 18

To earth I come 20

When the sun lights up the sky 23

MORNING SONGS

Birds in the air 23

From high upon the mountain 21

Morning is come 18

Rinca, ranca, rosy ray 19

Very early in the morning 22

EVENING POEMS

After my bath, I try, try, try 30

Before I jump into my bed 31

Lullabye, close thine eye 46

Lullabye, oh lullabye! 32

Softly wanders the evening wind 37

The owl cries loud: too-whit, too-whoo! 28

This is a baby ready for a nap 27

When cold winds blow 47

EVENING SONGS

At ev'ning when I go to bed 48
Birdies are flying away home to rest 40
Good angel, take me by the hand 41
Go to sleep now little darling 42
Hushaby, birdie, croon, croon 43
Hush, hush, my child, it's time to rest 30
Hush, my little child and do not weep 46
Hush! The waves are rolling in 38
I sail the silver moon path 36
Lulla-lulla-bye, my baby, close thine eye 34
Now cometh loving Mother Night 26
On tip toe comes the gentle dark 37
Sleep, baby sleep, I see two little sheep 33
Sleep, baby, sleep. Thy father minds the sheep 47
Sleep, my child, and sail away beyond the land of dreams . . 35
Sleep, my little mousey 32
Sleep, oh, Babushka mine 33
Slumber, little one, shoom-a-shy 31
Softly sighs the evening wind 27
The bright sun is sinking 44
The Lady Moon up yonder 28
Wee Willie Winkie runs through the town 45
Which is the way the wind blows over the silver sea . . . 29
Who has the nicest white sheep? 39

BIRTHDAY POEMS

Action Verses for Individual Children 55
A house the stars have built for me 52
When I have said my evening prayer 50

BIRTHDAY SONGS

In heaven shines a golden star 54
Kling, klang, gloria, rossel, rossel, filia 52
Let us all sweet music make 50

BIRTHDAY STORIES *(Index of titles)*

A Birthday Celebration in a Kindergarten 60
Birthday Story 60
Father Birthday 63

FAIRTYALE POEMS

A tired ass, too old to work 82
Briar Rosebud was a lovely child 67
By oak and ash and hawthorn tree 69
Morning dew and sunshine gold 85
On Midsummer Day, Jack climbed so high 86
Three little goats went walking 79
When the sun lights up the sky 66

FAIRYTALE SONGS

A little girl went in the wood 78
By night we work, we never shirk 69
Fee, Fi, Fo, Fum 86
From cloudlets and sky the eagles do fly 91
Gladly will I lend my hand 73
Hansel and Gretel went wand'ring o'er the wold . . . 88
Knock, knock, knock, please open the door 93
Little duck, little duck dost thou see 89
Milky-white, Milky-white, little cow, my beauty bright . . 87
Mother of the fairy tale 66
Now the ravens all are free 83

Of linen soft, of linen light 67
O Princess of the golden sun 90
Pull the thread and stitch the shoe 68
Rose of red and rose of white 85
Round about, round about, lo and behold 76
Sail away, silvern boat 77
Silver leaves are gleaming 71
Simpleton, so good and kind 75
Snow White and Rose Red, growing up so tall 84
Sweeping and cleaning and busy all day 80
The aged woman good and kind 79
Tip-a-tap, rip-a-rap, tik-a-tak-a-too! 68
Thru' the sunlit meadows and leafy glades we sing . . . 92
Walk along, skip along 74
We are the seven little gnomes 81
Whirring, softly whirring, turn, oh wheel of mine . . . 72
Up in the air I toss my ball 70

The Value of Music in the Life of the Young Child

Free Play in a Waldorf Kindergarten. It is a winter morning: the twenty children are busy with their work. The youngest, three- and four-year-olds, are helping the teacher chop apples for snack; some five-year-old girls are taking care of their "children" in the doll corner; next to them are a group of five-year-old boys and girls who are sitting at a round table polishing stones, grating chestnuts and chatting together. In the centre of the room an observant and energetic four-year-old boy is directing the six-year-olds in the construction of a snowplough: tables are stacked on each other, chairs turned upside down and leaned against the tables for the front part of the plough. A large basket of chestnuts is balanced on top of the plough. The chestnuts are grit and salt, to be scattered later on the ploughed streets. The room is small and the noise level is moderately high.

Underneath the windows, on the carpet where the children have a free space to build up scenes and play with standing puppets and animals, a six-year-old girl sits, absorbed in her work. She has laid out a forest of pine cones, which stands on the banks of a river of blue cloth. Stepping stones allow the poor shepherd boy, who lives at the edge of the forest, to cross the river and wind his way to the castle gates nearby . . . The princess, leaning out of her tower, sees him coming and calls down to him . . .

As she lays out the scene, the girl accompanies her actions with narrative, speaking in a soft tone, sometimes almost whispering to herself. When the puppets begin to live in the scene her voice changes, becoming more sung than spoken, the pitch of her spoken voice being taken over by her singing voice. Her recitative is not sing-song rhythmic, but the rhythm freely moves with the intention of the shepherd boy as he jumps from stone to stone. The pitch of the girl's voice is a colourful monotone: the pitch remains much the same, but the tone colour is enlivened through the intensity and quality of the words as the shepherd crosses the stream. There are moments when a word is spoken, then the narrative is sung again.

When the shepherd arrives at the castle gates, the princess calls down to him from her high tower. She is far away, and the girl reaches up with her voice to the distant place where the princess lives, and sings her greetings

9

down to the shepherd. The girl's voice is high now, but the intervals she sings are not large, they are between a third and a fifth. The high pitch of her voice, although it is not loud, has attracted some of the five-year-olds: several come over to the rug and lie on their stomachs, watching the play unfold. The shepherd now tells the princess of his wish that she come down and go with him. The simple recitative changes to a declamatory aria: a melody of several different tones arises, moving stepwise, the girl's voice becomes more intense as the shepherd pleads his cause. There is little repetition in the melody, but the movement contained in it provides a musical mood which waits expectantly for the princess's reply . . .

In the meantime, the snowplough has already cleared quite a few streets. It has come back to make a second round to scatter the grit and salt . . . The four-year-olds slicing apples jump up from the table. The noise of all those chestnuts hitting a wooden floor is so wonderful, they want to join the fun! The "mothers" putting their children to bed are angry that the snowplough has woken up their little ones, now the babies are crying . . . Some of the children polishing stones and grating chestnuts try throwing their stones and chestnuts on the floor – what a good idea, it makes a lovely *cracking* sound . . .

. . . the five-year-olds listening to the play hold their breaths as the princess agrees to go with the shepherd but he must first ask permission from her father, the king . . . The princess's instructions are sung to him in a melody of seconds with a strong, definite rhythm . . .

An observer can hardly believe that the chestnut-strewn chaos in the other half of the room (which the teacher is quickly helping to put right again) does not seem to penetrate the sheath of peacefulness which surrounds the puppet play. The children gathered around it show no sign that anything else in the room has taken place . . .

At the successful conclusion of the play, the children watching it lie still. The girl covers the scene with a cloth and sings in a half-whispering tone a farewell to the story of the shepherd and the princess. As her voice fades, there is a moment of absolute silence. Then the five-year-olds run back to the polishing table and the girl goes to the teacher to ask how long it will be until snack.

This description of a six-year-old girl's singing contains many elements of what has come to be called "Mood of the Fifth" music: the singing follows the rhythm of speech; melodies are simple, moving within intervals of seconds and thirds – sometimes as large as a fifth, rarely larger; melodies are often sung on one tone, the pitch taken from the speaking voice; the melodies are not written in major or in minor keys and have an open-ended feel to them. Above all is the mood of the music: when sung properly it seems to reach out and enfold the children in a protective sheath which has a quality of stillness and peace, although the children themselves may be active within it.

This music is a musical expression of an experience which is striven for in all aspects of Waldorf Education. It is difficult to describe in words, perhaps: "I am centred in my activity," "My thinking, feeling and willing are in balance." One feels deeply united with a task, at peace and yet still active. The young child finds this mood in play. S/he is deeply engaged in an activity which is then no longer interesting when the activity is over. The moment of silence at the end of the play was not a moment of reflection, but a moment which allowed the activity of watching the play to come to a complete end before the next task could engage the children's attention.

The broader context of this musical experience should be noted: the kindergarten just described is one where mood-of-the-fifth music was not cultivated by the teacher. The children learned only traditional children's songs and games which were sung in strict rhythm, and with major or minor key melodies. The six-year-old girl experienced similar music at home.

Yet the girl's singing is not an isolated or unusual musical event. Such singing can often be heard when a child's attention is fully engaged in his/her play. We grown-ups tend to dismiss such fragments of melody as noise, or incomplete attempts by the child to sing our music, not listening closely enough to discover the innate coherence of the child's activity. Too often well-meaning adults try to "correct" the pitch which is too high, or the rhythm which is irregular, and slowly wall in a living musicality with "proper" songs . . . Sooner or later, often at puberty, an attempt is made at breaking through these walls, as the pounding beat of popular music has long suggested.

The use of "Mood of the Fifth" music in the kindergarten encompasses two considerations. It is first of all a path of musical development for the adult, which schools his/her musical perception and ability so that s/he is able to participate in a musicality which the children *already possess*. This musicality may, for many reasons, lie dormant or misshapen within an individual child or group of children. Through the adult's use of Mood of the Fifth s/he can reawaken and bring back into movement the musicality which is so essential for the full development of the child's soul life. (To be labelled "unmusical" or "tone deaf" causes deep, lingering wounds to the child's self esteem. There are unfortunately many adults who can attest to the truth of this statement out of their own experience.)

Mood of the Fifth music can also help the adult to establish an additional point of contact with the child which shows him/her that the adult *understands*. One of the rewards of working with young children is surely the open look of delight on a child's face when s/he hears a story, plays a game, experiences something which pleases him/her. The look of delight means more, however, than just "I like that." On a deeper level it expresses the child's trust in the adult: "You know who I am, and what you offer me is that which I am searching for with my deepest intentions. I can follow you."

The present day task of the Waldorf Kindergarten is primarily a therapeutic one. It provides children with basic experiences which they need for healthy development, overcoming deficiencies which often occur today in the first years of life. A very large part of these experiences are sensory, as the development of the physical senses (touch, balance, etc.) lays the foundation for the later unfolding of the spiritual capacities (thinking, speech, etc.). The kindergarten is not a mirror of our daily lives, but an extract of the many activities, distilled to their essence. This provides a simplicity and basic necessity for the content of kindergarten life which the child can understand and imitate wholeheartedly. The meaningful activity around the child awakens his/her interest in the world, and this interest becomes the mainspring of later learning.

In the arts the materials presented to the child are restricted to essentials, and with these the child's imagination has free rein. This can be clearly seen, for example, in painting: the three primary colours are used – red, yellow and blue. The children are given watercolours, a large wet sheet of paper and a broad brush to paint with. The materials themselves preclude any precise drawing, colours flow into one another, sometimes mixing, sometimes remaining pure side by side. There is no right or wrong way of using the colours, the expansive, fiery or cool moods of the colours themselves guide the child's brush. The medium of water enables the child's soul to breathe freely in the movement of colour with the brush. If only the paper were bigger s/he could paint on and on . . .

Music can be approached in a similar way. Here as well the materials can be restricted so that the *activity* becomes of foremost importance. Only five different tones of our twelve tone system are used:

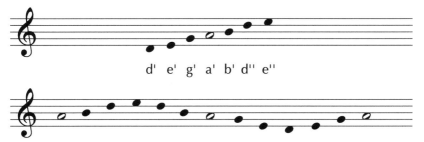

d' e' g' a' b' d'' e''

When a children's harp or lyre is used, the strings are tuned to pure fifths (like a violin's open strings) rather than the tempered intervals of the piano. The songs are not written in major or minor keys, but tend to circle around the middle tone, a'. The rhythm is free, either gently swinging (3 or 6 beats) or walking (2 or 4 beats), but the movement of the music takes its impulse from the words and seeks to accompany its inner content.

This style of music making lends itself wonderfully to the activities of circle time where movement, the spoken word and song freely flow from one to the other, just as the three basic colours do in painting. Teachers who have worked with Mood of the Fifth music in the classroom also know of its effectiveness in creating moments where the attention of all of the children is engaged, enabling a special mood to arise, whether in a puppet play, grace before meal, etc.

Newcomers to this music may at first experience difficulty in hearing the melodies or finding an inner connection to them. Others may have trouble finding the beginning pitch or singing the songs as high as they are written. None of these difficulties should be considered unsolvable problems.

Over time, the practice of Music of the Fifth songs often leads to a good sense of pitch. The voice gradually learns the placement of the tones, and the reduced number of tones make sight-singing possible even for the "unmusical" person.

Difficulty in reaching the higher notes (d", e"), which lie within traditional singing range of soprano and altos, can be due to breathing which is too shallow, as well as to the false idea that high notes are more difficult to sing and require greater effort. In the long run, the question of extending the vocal range is best addressed by an experienced teacher. But those without a teacher can still consider the following: the vocal range can be affected by physical movement. Often much can be accomplished by accompanying a song with large, simple, physical gestures. This helps free the breathing, allowing greater ease in reaching notes which are "too high." The songs can be practised with movement until the feeling of vocal mobility is secure. Then the outward movement can gradually become smaller and disappear altogether, all the while maintaining the inner freedom of movement in the voice.

An essential guide for adults who wish to find a path into the experience of Mood of the Fifth music can be found in Julius Knierim's *Songs in the Mood of the Fifth (Quintenlieder)*. This succinct and clearly written booklet describes, with simple exercises and musical examples, a path which really can be taken by all who have a sincere interest in further development of their musical abilities. By working with the suggestions contained in Julius Knierim's essay, the serious student can develop capacities which not only lead him/her into the musical world of the young child, but can help build a new relationship to traditional classical music, and to all further musical development.

Rudolf Steiner, in discussing music for the young child, spoke of the great importance of the Quintenstimmung = *Mood* of the Fifth. The suggestions mentioned in this article, and most especially in Dr. Knierim's book, are guideposts by which adults may find the way into this mood. They are not the mood itself. Individual observation, experimentation, and practice are the means by which the letter of the law may be enlivened by its spirit.

The goal of these booklets is to offer immediate practical help in working with young children. It is for this reason that a variety of musical styles is included. All songs (as well as stories and verses) have proved their worth in Waldorf kindergartens or other settings with young children. Some traditional tunes with new words have been included, and many traditional rhymes have been set to new melodies (either pentatonic or Mood of the Fifth). Familiar children's songs have been excluded for the most part because these are readily available in other collections. Most songs are set in D-pentatonic. This is done for pedagogical as well as practical reasons (see references). Experience has shown that many teachers and parents who wish to consciously address music-making with the young child are often just those who are themselves struggling with their own musical education. With most songs written in D-pentatonic mode (which are tones of a Choroi flute or children's harp, and are easy to play on a traditional recorder), it is hoped that the initial difficulties with note reading and transposition will be eased. The use of bar lines and time signatures varies, showing new possibilities of notation. Some songs have traditional time signatures, others have only a 3 or 4 at the beginning to indicate a more swinging or walking rhythm. The absence of bar lines leaves the singer free to determine the musical phrasing according to the rhythm of the words and their sense. Commas indicate a slight pause, or point of rest.

Jennifer Aulie

References:

Knierim, Julius. *Songs in the Mood of the Fifth 'Quintenlieder'.*
ISBN: 0 945803 14 1 (Rudolf Steiner College Press, California)

Steiner, Rudolf. *The Study of Man.*
ISBN: 0 85584 187 8 (Rudolf Steiner Press, England)

Steiner, Rudolf. *The Inner Nature of Music and the Experience of Tone.*
ISBN 0 88010 074 5 (Steiner Books, Massachusetts)

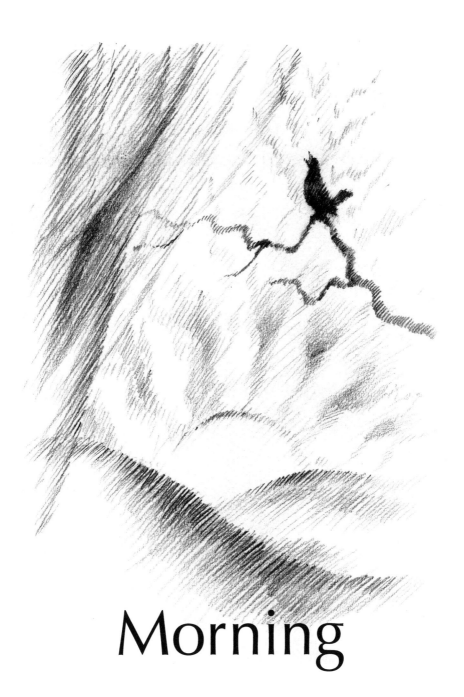

Morning

Morn-ing is come, night is a - way, We rise with the sun to wel-come the day.

N. Foster

Good morning, dear earth,
And good morning, dear sun.
Good morning, dear stones,
And flowers everyone.
Good morning, dear beasties
And birds on the tree.
Good morning to you
And good morning to me.

The moon on the one hand,
The sun on the other.
The moon is my sister,
The sun is my brother.
The moon on my left,
The sun on my right:
My brother good morning,
My sister good night.

H. Belloc

Rin - ca, ran - ca, ro - sy ray,

wel - come, wel - come gold - en day:

Win - dows o - pen wide,

light shall come in - side.

Oh sun, so bright:
Thou givest light
And warming love
From heaven above,
That life on earth
May come to birth.

Awake, the sun is shining bright:
He drives away the long, dark night.
The moon and stars have gone to rest
And earth in softest green is dressed.
Now will we open wide our heart:
Of this great world we all are part,
And if we work, or sleep, or play:
Be with us, golden sun, this day.

To earth I come
To greet the light,
To greet the sun,
The stones which rest,
The plants which grow,
The beasts which run,
To greet all men,
Who live and walk,
Who work and will,
Love God in all,
Then God greets me,
In all I do,
And I and you
In God are one.

Down is the earth.
Up is the sky.
There are my friends.
And here am I.

From Germany

From high up - on __ the moun - tain I

hear the sing - ing foun - tain: A -

wake, a - wake the sun shines bright, A -

wake to greet the gold - en light.

Cock-a-doodle-doo gets up with the sun.
"Wake up," he shouts, "the day has begun!"
Blackbird calls from the tall tree top,
And from their holes brown rabbits hop.
Cows to the meadow slowly go,
Ducks to the pond waddle all in a row.
Children wake up from their sleep,
And out of windows take a peep.
"Hello!" They call, "Come out to play!
Here's a brand new shining day."

From Germany

P. Patterson

Ver - y ear - ly in ___ the morn - ing
all the birds a - wake and sing,
Prais - ing God that now the sun his
warmth and light to earth will bring.

Early in the morning,
Oh hear the cock'rel call.
He struts about the farmyard
"Good morning, creatures all,"
He flaps his wings and sings to you
"Wake up now, cock-a-doodle-doo."

P. Patterson

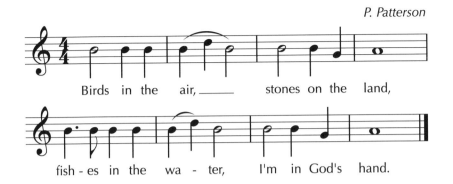

Birds in the air,_____ stones on the land,

fish - es in the wa - ter, I'm in God's hand.

When the sun lights up the sky
I sit right up and rub my eye.
I dress myself with greatest care.
I brush my teeth and comb my hair.
Then off to story time I go
To hear the stories that I love so.

The golden sun is shining
Up in the sky so blue:
Good morning, happy morning,
Good morning, sun, to you.

1. Take my brush,
   Take my broom,
   Clean and I clean
   Around my room;
   Clean and I clean
   Around my room
   To make it pretty and shiny-o.

2. Take my polish,
   Take my cloth,
   Rub and I rub
   And I polish it off;
   Rub and I rub
   And I polish it off
   To make it pretty and shiny-o.

3. Take my soap,
   Take my clothes,
   Down and down
   In the water they go;
   Down and down
   In the water they go
   To make them pretty and shiny-o.

4. Take my brush,
   Scrub my teeth,
   Scrubble and scrabble
   I brush my teeth;
   Bubble and blow
   Bubble and blow
   To make them pretty and shiny-o.

5. Tippy tappy toe
   I go to bed,
   Close my eyes
   I rest my head;
   Sleepy sleepy tight
   Sleepy sleepy tight
   To make them pretty and shiny-o.

W. *Guthrie*

Evening

M. Garff

P. Patterson

Now com - eth lov - ing Mo - ther
The flowers, she clo - ses soft and

Night and lays her man - tle
low, the wind she crad - les

o - ver the light: With lull - a -
to and fro:

bye a - sing - ing and ev' - ning

bells a - ring - ing, so close thine

eye, lull - a - bye, so close thine

eye, lull - a - bye.

This is a baby ready for a nap.
Lay him down in his mother's lap.
Cover him up so he won't peep.
Rock him till he's fast asleep.

W. Klein/H. Klole

Lyre:

Soft - ly sighs the even - ing wind, Through the moun - tains wend - ing.

Sleep - y birds now fold their wings, Now the day is

Lyre:

end - ing.

2. Little gnomes are sleepy too,
   Into their homes are creeping.
   Mid the tree roots deep below
   Soon they're soundly sleeping.

The owl cries loud: too-whit, too-whoo!
'Tis night, 'tis night, the door shut tight,
The day's work is done for everyone.
So now good night, good night, good night!

From Germany

A. *Gladstone*   *P. Patterson*

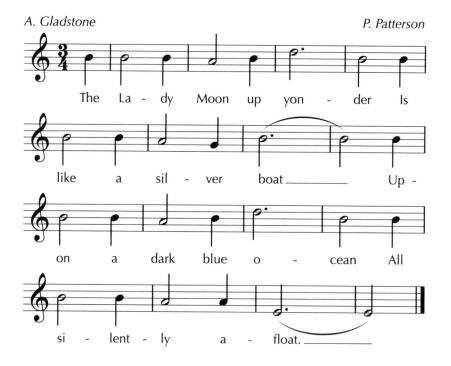

The La - dy Moon up yon - der Is

like a sil - ver boat____ Up -

on a dark blue o - cean All

si - lent - ly a - float.____

2. And when the fairies waken
   They climb the moonbeams white
   And far across the heavens
   Go sailing in the night.

From Holland   J. Aulie

Which is the way the wind ____ blows
o - ver the sil - ver sea,
Bring-ing a ship for fa - ther and a
gold - en dream __ for me?

2. Which is the way the wind blows over the silver sea,
   Bringing a gown for mother and a silver shoe for me?

3. Which is the way the wind blows over the silver sea,
   Bringing a moon for mother and a tiny star for me?

P. Patterson

Hush, hush, my child, it's time to rest, The
birds have set - tled in their nest. The
moon sails high, she shines so bright, On
fields so still the snow lies white.

After my bath, I try, try, try
To wipe myself till I'm dry, dry, dry.
Hands to wipe, and fingers and toes,
And two wet legs and a shiny nose.
Just think, how much less time I'd take,
If I were a dog, and could shake, shake, shake.

Before I jump into my bed,
Before I dim the light,
I put my shoes together,
So they can talk at night.
I'm sure they would be lonesome,
If I tossed one here and there,
So I put them close together,
For they're a friendly pair.

M. Meyerkort

P. Patterson

Slum - ber, lit - tle one, shoom - a - shy,

Stars are shin - ing ___ in the sky,

Stars a - round you gleam and glow, In

fruit and flow - er, In crys - tal and snow. So

slum - ber lit - tle one, shoom - a - shy.

M. Meyerkort
P. Patterson

Sleep, my lit - tle mou - sey,

sleep the whole night through,

Till the cock in his house - y calls his

cock - a - doo - dle - doo!

Lullabye, oh lullabye!
Flowers are closed and men are sleeping.
Lullabye, oh lullabye!
Stars are up, the moon is peeping.
Lullabye, oh lullabye!
While the birds are silent keeping.
Lullabye, oh lullabye!
Sleep my baby all a-sleeping.
Lullabye, oh lullabye!

M. Meyerkort

P. Patterson

Sleep, ba-by sleep, I see two lit-tle sheep:
one is black and one is white, if you do not
sleep to-night, first the black and then the white will
give your lit - tle toes a bite.

From Russia

Traditional Russian

Sleep, oh, Bab-ush-ka mine, cold winds are wail-ing,
Warm is thy cra-dle nest, soft as the snow.

2. Sleep then, Babushka mine, daylight is failing,
   Bright on thy cradle nest firelight will glow.

From Austria

Traditional Austrian

Lul - la - lul - la - bye, my

ba - by, close thine eye,

eye. With bells and flutes and

lyres a - ring - ing An - gels fill the

sky with sing - ing. Lul - la - lul - la -

bye, my ba - by close thine eye.

C. Petrash

C. Petrash

Sleep, my child, and sail a - way Be -
yond the land of dreams, _____ Your
an - gel guides your ship up - on The
sil - ver sea of sleep, _____ You'll
come once more at jour - ney's end To your
heav'n - ly home of gold, _____ The
sun will wake you in the morn, A
new day shall un - fold. _____

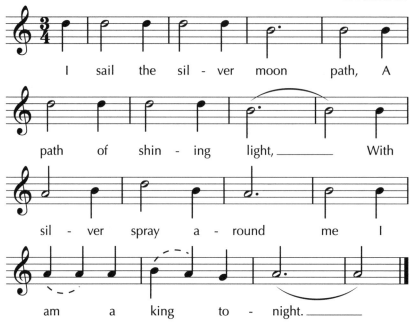

I sail the sil - ver moon path, A

path of shin - ing light, _____ With

sil - ver spray a - round me I

am a king to - night. _____

2. I sail the silver moon path,
   The silver is my own,
   The shining stars will guide me,
   The crest of the wave is my throne.

J. Aulie

On tip - toe comes the gen - tle dark

(hmm) _____ to help the child - ren sleep,

And si - lent - ly on sil - ver paths

(hmm) _____ the slum - ber fair - ies creep.

1. Softly wanders the evening wind,
   Brightly shines the moon,
   Homeward bound are little gnomes
   Upon their silver shoon.

2. Seek now for their little house
   Under the yellow thatch,
   Fall asleep on mossy bed,
   Little Pinch and Patch.

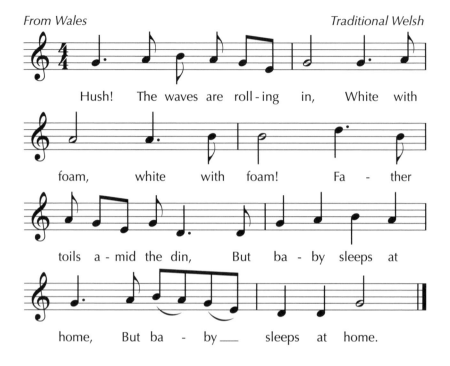

Hush! The waves are roll-ing in, White with foam, white with foam! Fa - ther toils a-mid the din, But ba - by sleeps at home, But ba - by ___ sleeps at home.

2. Hush! The winds roar load and deep,
   On they come, on they come,
   Brother seeks the wandering sheep
   But baby sleeps at home,
   But baby sleeps at home.

3. Hush! The rain sweeps o'er the house,
   Where they roam, where they roam,
   Sister goes to seek the cows
   But baby sleeps at home,
   But baby sleeps at home.

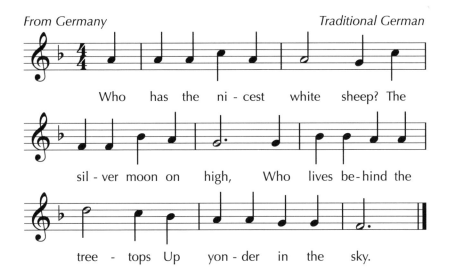

Who has the ni-cest white sheep? The sil-ver moon on high, Who lives be-hind the tree-tops Up yon-der in the sky.

2. She comes late in the evening
   When everyone's asleep,
   So slow and calm she wanders
   Across the heaven's deep.

3. All night she guards her white flocks
   In meadows blue and deep,
   For all the little twinkling stars,
   Are only her white sheep.

From Wales *Traditional Welsh*

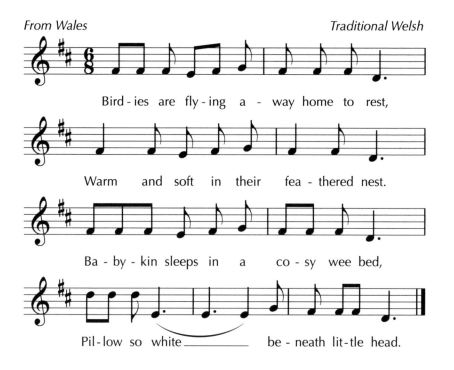

Bird - ies are fly - ing a - way home to rest,

Warm and soft in their fea - thered nest.

Ba - by - kin sleeps in a co - sy wee bed,

Pil - low so white _____ be - neath lit - tle head.

2. Come, my sweet babykin, dear little one,
   Say goodnight to the big red sun.
   He will come back when the darkness has gone,
   Babykin, too, will wake with the dawn.

G. Hayn

P. Patterson

Good an - gel, take me by ___ the hand and lead me through the star - ry land. Stars sing to me while I'm a - sleep, your lov - ing watch for - ev - er keep, That when I wake through all my days, I may glad - ly fol - low in God's own ways.

41

U. Grahl   U. Grahl

Go   to   sleep   now   lit - tle   dar - ling,

Night   is   com - ing   blue   and   deep,

Stars   are   bright   and   an - gels   car - ry

Down   from   heav - en   ho - ly   sleep.

Aa   -   ai - aa,   aa   -   ai - aa,

Down   from   heav - en   ho - ly   sleep.

2.   Slumber sweetly, little darling,
     Night has come so blue and deep.
     Weaving dreams of silver starlight,
     Angels guard thy holy sleep.
     Aa-ai-aa, aa-ai-aa,
     Angels guard thy holy sleep.

42

Hush - a - by, bird - ie, croon, croon,

hush - a - by, bird - ie, croon. _____ The

sheep are gane to the sil - ver wood and the

cows are gane to the broom; broom, and its

braw milk-ing the kye, kye, and it's

braw milk - ing the kye. _____ The

birds are sing - ing, the bells are ring-ing, the

wild deer come gal - lop-ing by, by.

Traditional   *J. Aulie*

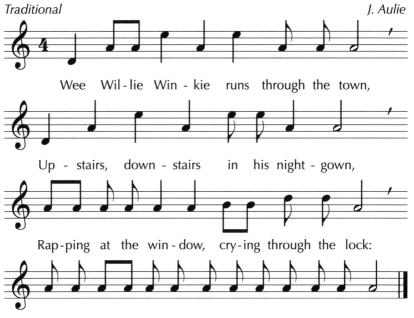

Wee   Wil-lie   Win-kie   runs   through   the   town,

Up - stairs,   down - stairs   in   his   night - gown,

Rap-ping   at   the   win - dow,   cry-ing   through   the   lock:

"Are the child-ren in their beds for now it's eight o' clock?"

From Germany   *P. Patterson*

Hush, my lit-tle child and do not weep, The sun has gone, it's time to sleep. The clock strikes twelve, bright shines the moon, Sleep well, the morn - ing will come soon.

1. Lullabye, close thine eye,
   Aya, ay,
   Birds now sing a song for thee,
   Sing it in the dreamland tree.
   Lullabye, close thine eye,
   Aya, ay.

2. Lullabye, close thine eye,
   Aya, ay,
   Butterfly in sunshine gold,
   Flies with you to mother's fold.
   Lullabye, close thine eye,
   Aya, ay.

From Germany

46

From Germany   J. Aulie

Sleep, ba - by, sleep. Thy fa - ther minds the sheep. Thy mo - ther shakes the dream-land tree, A lit-tle dream then falls on thee. Sleep, ba - by sleep.

2. Sleep, baby, sleep.
   The large stars are the sheep.
   The little ones are lambs so small,
   The moon a shepherd guarding all.
   Sleep, baby, sleep.

When cold winds blow,
And bring us snow,
At night what I like most
Is to climb in bed
And hide my head
And sleep as warm as toast.

"Shhhhhh – good night!"

At ev' - ning when I go __ to bed, I
see the stars shine o - ver - head,
They are the lit - tle dais - ies white, That
dot the mea - dow of __ the night.

2. And often when I'm dreaming so
   Across the sky the moon will go,
   She is a lady sweet and fair
   Who comes to gather daisies there.

3. For when at morning I arise
   There's not a star left in the skies;
   She's picked them all and dropped them down
   Into the meadows of the town.

Birthdays

VERSE OF ANTICIPATION

When I have said my evening prayer,
And my clothes are folded on the chair.
And mother switches off the light,
I'll still be five years old tonight.

But, from the very break of day,
Before the children rise and play,
Before the greenness turns to gold,
Tomorrow, I'll be six years old.

Six kisses when I wake,
Six candles on my cake.

A. Gladstone

P. Patterson

Let us all sweet mus - ic make
as each o - ther's hand we take, We
dance and sing, with joy we see the
prince is on his way to me. The

Continued...

prince, he comes a - rid - ing by,

trot, trot, trot he gal - lops high, A -

round and round the pal - ace ground un -

til the prin - cess he has found.

O - pen the win - dows far and wide, we

ask the prince to come in - side, He

bows so low, for it is plain the

prin - cess he has found a - gain.

1. A house the stars have built for me,
   Of silver tones and gold,
   From many windows I can see
   What once the angels told.

2. To find on earth in human hearts,
   In flowers, beasts and stones
   The gift the sun to earth imparts,
   Its own life-giving tones.

3. In ev'ry deed I hear them sing,
   Below and up above,
   For all that unto earth I bring,
   I give them back my love.

F. Geuter

Continued...

mai-den of the flow - er!" "To her I want to go." "No, no, no! She can not see the light of day, un - less you break the stones a - way." "First stone, se - cond stone, third stone, you go with me home.

Suggested directions: *Between 2 and 4 princesses sit on the floor in the centre of the ring. Between 2 and 4 princes join hands and walk around the outside of the circle. At 'No, no, no!' the circle contracts to stand closely around the princesses. At 'First stone' the first prince pats one child on the shoulder, then a second and a third. If the circle is small, only the third 'stone' will follow the prince; if large all three stones will follow him, holding hands. So: the inner circle dissolves, while a new one is formed. The very last tine sing 'Yes, yes, yes,' instead of 'No, no, no,' and then the verse is finished to 'la, la, la,' while the princes and princesses dance in the middle and the circle clap hands.*

N. Foster

In heav - en shines a gold - en star, An
an - gel led me from a - far, From
heav - en high un - to the earth, And
brought me to my house of birth.

2. Welcome, welcome lovely day
   With flowers bright and sunshine gay,
   With painted birds that sing their song
   And make me kind and good and strong.

Action Verses for Individual Children

Used in impromptu birthday plays

1. Down I'll go
   Firm and slow
   Down to earth
   Into birth.

2. I have chosen this day
   For to come to the earth.
   I will lighten your way
   To the Christ Child's birth.

3. I have come to birth,
   I stand on the earth:
   My love to all I'll give,
   With courage I will live.

4. Little Angel, fly,
   Fly down from the sky,
   Come into our arm,
   We will hold you warm.

5. The heavens high
   Are blue so blue
   Like Mary's mantle in the sky
   To shelter you.

6. With helmet gold
   With heart so bold
   Ride forth, now, ride
   The world is wide.

7. Summer rose, summer rose,
   Brings light and warmth
   Wherever she goes.

8. Awake from cold and night
   I bring you warmth and light.

9. Lift your head and wear your crown,
   Lift your foot and place it down.

10. You and I, I and you
    We will seek the Christ Child too.

11. Joy and laughter you may bring
    To everyone and everything.

12. I dance with the flowers,
    I sing with the sun,
    The warmth of my heart,
    I bring everyone.

13. Receive the light, it comes from high;
    So let it shine on all you try.

14. On earth I now stand,
    I stretch out my hand
    To greet you, my friend.
       All your hand will do and bring,
       Like music of the stars shall sing.

15. I am the Prince of Spring,
    I make the flowers ring,
    I make the birdies sing,
    And all I have, my wealth, my fun,
    I like to share with everyone.
       With Jenny I'll share
       My gifts so fair.
    Now let's enjoy together
    The flowers, birds and sunny weather.

16. Look up! St. Michaël to see,
    He watches day and night.
    Then go! The servant for to be
    Of Michaël, the angel bright.

17. Every word I speak
    Is a flaming light,
    Every word I sing
    Warms me in the night.

18. Deep in my little shell below
    Hidden treasures glow.
    I take them to the light of day
    To brighten up the way.

19. Stars work down on land and sea,
    Stars work also into me.
        So fingers and feet
        Are nimble and neat.

20. Round and round I wind my way
    As in my house I hide.
    Treasures I take to light of day,
    Then open doorway wide.

21. Treasures fair I hold,
    Will share with everyone.
    One, two, three I go
    Until my task I've done.

22. Winds bring greetings from the sky
    As soft into my house they fly.
    I take greetings far and wide,
    Knock on the door, bring joy inside.
        The wind is my brother,
        We love one another.

23. A house the stars have built for me
Of silver tones and gold,
Then come inside with one, two, three,
To share the gifts I hold.

24. Snowflakes are falling,
Snowflakes are calling.
Lo, the snowdrops listen well,
Ring their little snowdrop bell.

25. My house is all a-glow
To warm you so.

26. Then swing on high
To seek the secrets in the sky.

27. Living light of stars above,
Crystal light below.
Light your lantern with your love,
Let it glow and glow.

28. Stars shine high, stars shine low,
Weave your deeds both to and fro.

29. Flowers and fruits they come and go,
Stars you'll find always at home.

30. Take the gold from far and wide,
Take it down and right inside.

31. Golden in the garden
Like the golden sun,
So we walk the winter way,
Warming everyone.

32. Starry light is guiding night and day,
Starry music lives in every word I say.

33. Here we build in meadow green,
    Build a throne for the Flower Queen.
        Scatter flowers here and there,
        Scatter flowers everywhere.

34. Amy can see far
    Like a crystal star.
        And I can take your hand
        To lead you into winterland.

Verses 1 to 34 inclusive,
M. Meyerkort

35. Roses round the garden
    Make a ruby ring,
    They drink up summer's fire
    To warm you like a king.

B. Summers

36. The stars all whisper softly
    To all of us each night,
    Like angels in the darkness
    Who guide you with their light.

B. Summers

A Birthday Celebration in a Kindergarten

When the birthday morning came the children took off their coats and waited in the hall. The birthday child and his mother and father sat down while the other children joined hands and, when quiet, were led into the Kindergarten. They were led to sit on their chairs in the form of a large circle. The birthday table, prepared by the teacher the evening before, stood in the centre of the circle. On the mantelpiece, at one end of the room, burnt two candles: on one side the tall Festival Candle and on the other side a smaller candle held by a hand-carved wooden angel which was lit every morning at ring time. Two chairs in front of the mantelpiece were kept empty. When the children were ready and quiet the Kindergarten teacher walked into the hall and singing the birthday song, led parents and birthday child once around the circle of children. With a gesture of the hand she invited mother and father to sit down. Child and teacher remained standing in front of the mantelpiece, a little outside the circle of chairs, facing the circle. The teacher began to tell the story:

Birthday Story

Once upon a time there was a Big Angel and a Little Angel. Big Angel led Little Angel from house to house. Little Angel worked in the house of the Sun. He worked in the house of the Moon and in the houses of the many Stars. When he had finished his work in each house, Little Angel received a gift. One day Little Angel said, "I want to work on the earth." – "Yes," replied Big Angel, "it is time for you to go to the earth. I will take care of your wings until you return, because now you will become a human child."

Then Big Angel took the gifts of Sun, Moon and Stars and changed them into sounds, tones, music. "When you are on the earth," said Big Angel, "you will hear the music of these gifts in the sound of your name, and that will give you strength in the tasks you have chosen to do on the earth."

The teacher lit the white candle on a gilded stick, which she held by her side, from the angel candle on the mantelpiece and held it with a meaningful gesture in front of her.

"Goodbye, Little Angel." – "Goodbye, Guardian Angel." And with the gifts of Sun, Moon and Stars sounding in and around him the little one went down the rainbow bridge.

Teacher and birthday child slowly walked a few steps forward.

He/She went to the house in which he wanted to prepare his new work. And there a mother and a father were waiting for him.

Teacher with her one free arm lifted the child onto his mother's lap.

Mother and father were overjoyed that a child had come who wanted their care and they said: "His name is . . . . . ."

The teacher lowered the stick with the candle and lit the Light of Life candle, the slightly larger candle in the centre of the cake which stood in the middle of the birthday table. And as she lit the Light of Life candle the teacher softly repeated: ". . . . . . , is his name."

The teacher, holding the candlestick in front of her, walked a large circle inside the circle of chairs telling three to five incidents, experiences (e.g., feeding, sitting, crawling, first step, etc.,) out of the first year of the birthday child's life, as she had ascertained them from the parents a few days previously. Having finished walking the circle the teacher lit the first smaller white candle on the carved wooden ring around the birthday cake with the words:

And . . . . . was one year old.

The teacher holding the candlestick in front of her walked a narrower circle inside the circle of chairs telling three to five incidents, experiences (e.g., first walking, first speaking, having a bath, emptying out daddy's waste paper basket, etc.,) out of the second year of the birthday child's life as she had ascertained them from the parents a few days previously. Having completed this narrower circle the teacher lit the second smaller white candle on the carved wooden ring around the birthday cake with the words:

And . . . . . was two years old.

The teacher continued walking ever narrower circles as she told a few episodes out of subsequent years in the child's life and she lit one candle after another, until all had been lit.

At the end of her last round the teacher said:

And today . . . . . is six years old.

The teacher held the candlestick out to the mother who blew out the flame and the teacher put the candlestick away. Everyone sang first the birthday song and then the well known song: "Happy Birthday To You." Parents and birthday child went to the birthday table and looked at the cards and presents the children and teacher had made and brought. The birthday child blew out the candles, opened the curtains, said goodbye to his parents and the morning proceeded as usual.

When after procedures in the cloakroom the children returned into the Kindergarten for mid-morning lunch the birthday child found flowers around his plate and the birthday cake, with candles lit, on the table. After singing 'Grace,' he cut the cake and handed it round to the other children.

At lunchtime when the children stood in the ring form to sing goodbye, the birthday child fetched a basket and packed everything from the birthday table into it. He stood in the middle of the ring with the basket in his arms while the children and the teacher sang the goodbye song. Next morning he returned the empty basket.

M. Meyerkort

Father Birthday

Once upon a time there was an old man. He lived in a log hut deep in the wood.

A long time ago, his grandchildren had come to the hut to visit him. They had planted fir trees around his hut. The trees had grown and grown tall and taller, so that now they were taller than the hut.

The old man lived happily in his hut. But one day his eyes were sad. Tomorrow was his birthday and he would be all on his own.

In the evening, he sat in front of the fire and watched the flames, thinking about the time when he was a little boy. Then he had woken early in the morning and heard his mother sing to him and he always had a birthday cake with white candles on it. On one birthday there was a small gift. He did not know who had given it to him and when he asked his father he was told that this gift must have come from Father Birthday.

The old man smiled a little smile. He watched the flames of the fire turn the wood into ashes: "Time for my bed," he said. He slipped on his nightshirt and put on his night cap, pulling it right down over his ears. He said his prayers, then got into bed. Soon he fell asleep.

Very early in the morning, the old man stirred. He opened his eyes. Something was shining near his bed. Yes! There was something on his table. It was a white candle. He sat up and looked at it. Something else was there too. A white egg lay beside the candle.

The old man was wide awake now.

"Today is my birthday," he said. "Where could this candle and this egg have come from?"

But first the stove had to be fed. The old man went into the forest and gathered wood, to bring it home to his hut. He stoked up the fire and soon it was hot enough to bake the cake.

Carefully the old man cracked the egg. He took some butter, sugar and flour and mixed them well with his wooden spoon. He spread the mixture in the tin and put it in the oven. Soon it was baked enough. Not too much. Not too little. It was just right! He covered it and left it to cool.

All day he kept the white candle burning. In the evening he placed the cake on the hearth beside the fire.

Then the old man looked into the flames. A smile spread over his face. "It must have been Father Birthday who came to me this morning."

He broke a piece of cake for himself. Then he broke off another piece and placed it on the hearth.

A. Hope

Fairytales

From Hungary P. Patterson

Mo - ther of ____ the fair - y tale
Sail me in ____ your sil - ver boat,

take me by your sil - ver hand,
sail me si - lent - ly a - float.

Mo - ther of ____ the fair - y tale

take me to ____ your shin - ing land.

When the sun lights up the sky
I sit right up and rub my eyes.
I dress myself with greatest care.
I brush my teeth and comb my hair.
Then off to Story House I go,
To hear the stories that I love so.

THE STAR CHILD

From Germany   *P. Patterson*

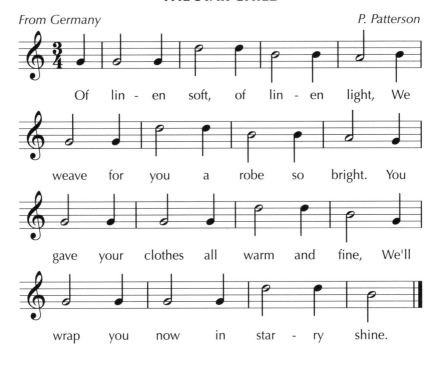

Of lin - en soft, of lin - en light, We weave for you a robe so bright. You gave your clothes all warm and fine, We'll wrap you now in star - ry shine.

BRIAR ROSE

Briar Rosebud was a lovely child.
We pray, dear Rosebud, take great care.
Here comes a wicked fairy now.
Briar Rosebud sleep a hundred years.
The thorny hedge grows thick and tall.
The noble prince comes riding by.
He takes his sword and cuts it down.
Briar Rosebud wake and rise again.
We'll all go to the wedding feast.
Then let us sing and dance with glee.

From Germany

THE GOBLIN COBBLERS

P. Patterson

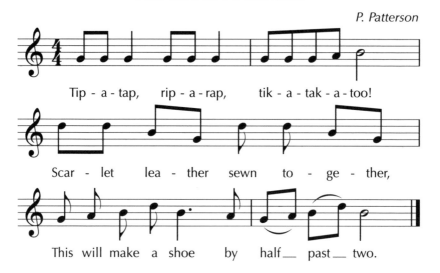

Tip - a - tap, rip - a - rap, tik - a - tak - a - too!

Scar - let lea - ther sewn to - ge - ther,

This will make a shoe by half __ past __ two.

THE GOBLIN COBBLERS

P. Patterson

Pull the thread and stitch the shoe,

Pull it tight and that will do.

Fair - y __ fin - gers nim - ble light,

First the left shoe then the right.

P. Patterson

By night we work, we ne - ver shirk with

nee - dle and thim - ble and thread. _____ The

cob-bler's a - sleep, he must not peep but

stay tucked in - side his soft bed, _____ But

stay tucked in - side his soft bed. _____

THE GOBLIN COBBLERS

By oak and ash and hawthorn tree
Come all elves and so come we.
Moonbeams light us on our way,
We work by night and sleep by day.

69

THE FROG PRINCE

M. Meyerkort   *P. Patterson*

Up in the air I toss my ball,

Back in my hand it will fall and fall,

Fly gold - en ball fly high, so high,

Shine lit - tle sun, shine in the sky.

ONE-EYE, TWO-EYES, THREE-EYES

N. Nicholson

P. Patterson

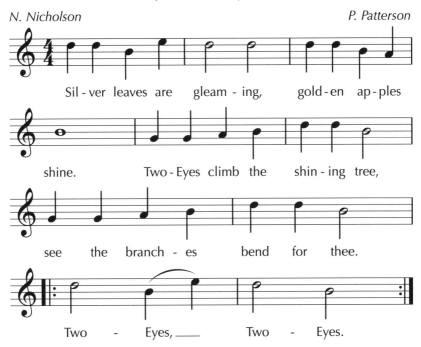

Sil - ver leaves are gleam - ing, gold - en ap - ples shine. Two - Eyes climb the shin - ing tree, see the branch - es bend for thee. Two - Eyes, ___ Two - Eyes.

GOLDEN MARY AND PITCH MARY (MOTHER HOLLE)

M. Meyerkort

Whir - ring, soft - ly whir - ring,
Swift - ly, deft - ly turn - ing,

Turn, oh wheel of mine.
Spin a thread so fine.

Thus I sing and gent - ly tread and
Spin a long and gold - en thread and

Spin __ a long and gold - en thread.

GOLDEN MARY AND PITCH MARY (MOTHER HOLLE)

From Germany

P. Patterson

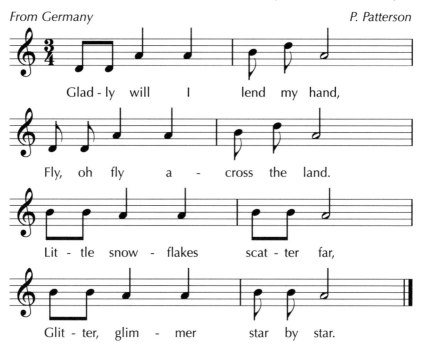

Glad - ly will I lend my hand,

Fly, oh fly a - cross the land.

Lit - tle snow - flakes scat - ter far,

Glit - ter, glim - mer star by star.

THE GOLDEN GOOSE

J. Marcus   *J. Marcus*

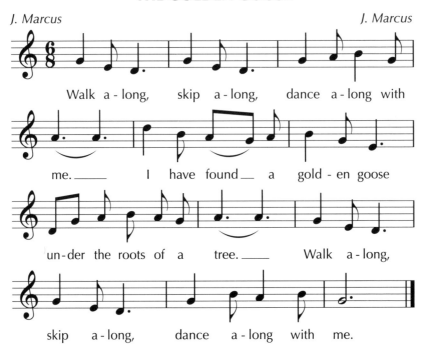

Walk a - long, skip a - long, dance a - long with

me. _____ I have found _ a gold - en goose

un - der the roots of a tree. _____ Walk a - long,

skip a - long, dance a - long with me.

THE GOLDEN GOOSE

Sim - ple-ton, so good and kind, A
won - drous gold - en goose did find, His
ship on land and sea did ride, And
so at last he won his bride.

P. Patterson

Round a-bout, round a-bout, lo and be - hold.

Wheel a-way, wheel a-way, straw in - to gold.

Ding - a - ding, ding - a - ding, ding - a - dee,

Ring - a - ring, ring - a - ring, ring - a - ree.

Oh what fun, _____ gold I've spun,

and a ring I've won. _____

2. Round about, round about, lo and behold.
Wheel away, wheel away straw into gold.
Ding a ding, ding a ding, ding a dee,
Ring a ring, ring a ring, ring a ree.
Oh what fun,
Gold I've spun,
And a chain I've won.

Continued...

3. Round about, round about, lo and behold.
   Wheel away, wheel away, straw into gold.
   Ding a ding, ding a ding, ding a dee,
   Ring a ring, ring a ring, ring a ree.
   Oh what fun,
   Gold I've spun,
   And a child I've won.

THE TWELVE DANCING PRINCESSES

A. Gladstone

P. Patterson

Sail a - way, sil - vern boat,

On the wa - ter gent - ly float,

Through the ma - gic moon - lit vale, With -

out an oar, with - out a sail.

Sail a - way!

THE SWEET PORRIDGE

J. Marcus   *J. Marcus*

2. She met an old wise woman there,
   Tra-la-la-la-la,
   Who gave a cooking pot to her,
   Tra-la-la-la-la.

3. When you are hungry then you say,
   Cook, little pot, cook.
   When you've had enough you say,
   Stop, little pot, stop,
   Stop, little pot, stop.

N. Foster

The a - ged wo - man good and kind, The
lit - tle girl in the wood did find, Now
all have had e - nough to eat.
Stop! Lit - tle pot, stop! _____

Three little goats went walking
One lovely summer's day.
They crossed a bridge to get some grass
But a troll got in their way.
They tricked the troll and down he fell
Into the water wet.
Now three little goats are getting fat
And the troll hasn't come back yet.

SNOW WHITE AND THE SEVEN DWARFS

W. Braithwaite

P. Patterson

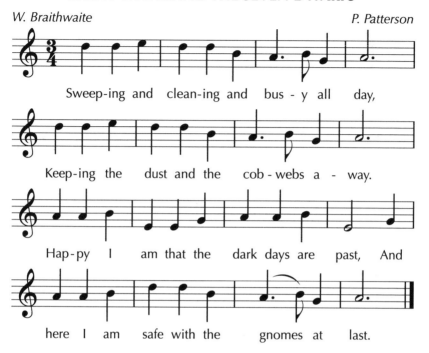

Sweep-ing and clean-ing and bus - y all day,

Keep-ing the dust and the cob - webs a - way.

Hap-py I am that the dark days are past, And

here I am safe with the gnomes at last.

2. Eight little places for them and for me,
   Tumblers a-shining as bright as can be.
   Polish each chair for each little man
   And now to get ready as quick as I can.

3. Washing of trousers and mending of socks,
   Oh what big holes they get climbing the rocks!
   Here is my needle and here is my thread,
   There's plenty to do 'ere they come home to bed.

A. *Gladstone*

P. Patterson

We   are the se - ven   lit - tle gnomes,   The

crag - gy   moun - tains   are   our   homes,   We

work   from   morn   till   night.   With

ham - mers   work   we   knock, knock, knock,   A -

gainst   the   sol - id   rock, rock, rock,

To   seek   the   trea - sures   bright._____

TOWN MUSICIANS OF BREMEN

1. A tired ass, too old to work,
   Went from his home one day.
   A great musician I will be,
   He to himself did say.

2. And on his way he met a dog
   Who had been turned out too.
   Oh come with me and sing with me
   I'll show you what to do.

3. The dog got up and followed him
   And soon they met a cat.
   My mistress does not want me now
   What do you think of that?

4. Oh come with us and sing with us,
   The ass and dog replied.
   Then on the way the three of them
   An anxious cock espied.

5. Oh come, be one of us, my friend,
   Don't let it get you down,
   We're off to earn our living now,
   Make music in the town.

6. They travelled on together
   Till far into the night,
   And from the darkness of the wood
   They saw a little light.

7. They looked into the window
   To see what was within:
   A band of robbers seated round
   A feast fit for a king.

Continued...

8. They soon thought of a splendid plan
   To get the robbers out:
   They all would sing together
   With a great and mighty shout.

9. The robbers were so terrified
   They ran with might and main,
   That spitting, screeching, barking - o
   They dared not face again.

10. So now the brave musicians
    At last have found a home,
    And there they must be living still,
    If they be not dead and gone.

C. Thatcher

THE SEVEN RAVENS

N. Foster

N. Foster

Now the ra - vens all are free,

Hu-mans a - gain they all may be,

Saved by their sis - ter, true and brave, Who

jour-neyed so far, her bro-thers to save.

SNOW WHITE AND ROSE RED

J. Patterson

P. Patterson

Snow White and Rose Red, grow-ing up ___ so tall, Like the ros - es in the gar - den 'gainst your mo - ther's wall. Lit - tle dwarf has caught his beard, snip, snap, snee, Use your scis - sors set him free, snip, snap, snee, snip - per, snap - per, snee.

SNOW WHITE AND ROSE RED

A. Gladstone   *N. Foster*

Rose of red and rose of white,

Child of love and child of light,

In a wreath your flow - ers twine,

Through the win - ter's gloom to shine.

2.   Rose of red and rose of white,
Child of love and child of light.
In a wreath your flowers entwine,
White as bread and crimson wine.

SNOW WHITE AND ROSE RED

Morning dew and sunshine gold
Over heath and forest,
Catch the little silver fish
For our Mother dearest.

Foxglove pink and harebell blue
In the meadow sunny,
Butterflies of shining hue
Seek the golden honey.

From Germany

JACK AND THE BEANSTALK

Traditional

J. Aulie

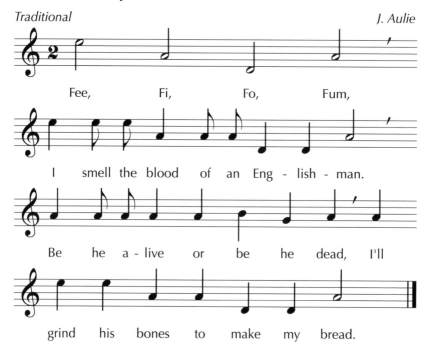

Fee, Fi, Fo, Fum,

I smell the blood of an Eng - lish - man.

Be he a - live or be he dead, I'll

grind his bones to make my bread.

JACK AND THE BEANSTALK

On Midsummer Day, Jack climbed so high,
He mounted the beanstalk right into the sky,
To the home of the giant so heavy and tall
Who stole Jack's treasures and hid them all.
Jack brought back the hen that laid eggs of gold,
And money bags filled with wealth untold,
And the magic harp that so sweetly sings,
With no one having to pluck the strings.
Now Jack has cut down the beanstalk so high,
The giant has fallen down from the sky,
And we are so happy, so happy and gay,
For the giant is dead this Midsummer Day.

G. Sargeant

JACK AND THE BEANSTALK

P. Patterson

P. Patterson

Milk - y - white,   Milk - y - white,

lit - tle cow,   my   beau - ty bright,

Come   and give   your   milk   so cream - y.

Milk - y - white   so   kind   and dream - y,

Lit - tle cow, my beau - ty bright,   Milk - y - white!

2. Milky-white, Milky-white, little cow, my beauty bright,
   Come with me, you cannot stay,
   You must help a different way.
   Little cow, my beauty bright, Milky-white!

HANSEL AND GRETEL

From Germany   *J. Aulie*

Han - sel and Gre - tel went
Dark was the for - est and

wand' - ring o'er the wold. They
bit - ter, bit - ter cold.

found a lit - tle house made of

cake and sug - ar clear. Come now, says Han -

sel, who can be liv - ing here?

2. See, now a witch opens up the doorway wide,
   Asking the children to follow her inside.
   She offers them red apples with sugar, nuts and milk,
   Covers two beds then with linen and with silk.

3. Early next morn they are roused from their sleep
   Hansel is locked in a stable dark and deep.
   And Gretel must fetch water and set a fire alight.
   See, now the witch she rejoices with delight.

Continued...

4. Wicked old witch wants to see the fire roar,
   Gretel she pushes her and shuts the oven door.
   Then quickly to the stable dear Gretel makes her way,
   Draws back the door-bolt and out comes Hansel gay.

5. Home, now the children are wandering o'er the wold.
   Laden with crystals and precious stones and gold.
   To welcome back his children their father was so gay
   And if they've not died, then they're living still today.

HANSEL AND GRETEL

M. Meyerkort   P. Patterson

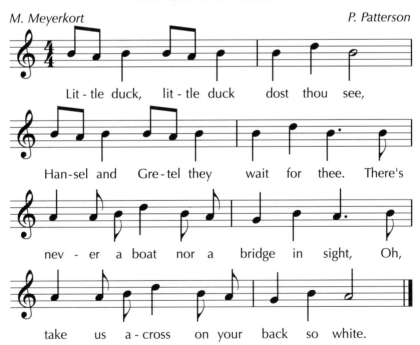

Lit - tle duck, lit - tle duck dost thou see,

Han-sel and Gre-tel they wait for thee. There's

nev - er a boat nor a bridge in sight, Oh,

take us a - cross on your back so white.

THE CRYSTAL BALL

M. Bucknall   *P. Patterson*

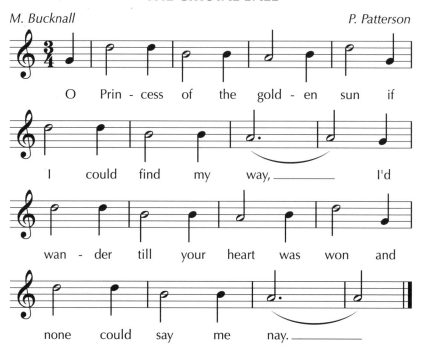

O Prin - cess of the gold - en sun if
I could find my way, _____ I'd
wan - der till your heart was won and
none could say me nay. _____

THE FLOWER QUEEN'S DAUGHTER

M. Bucknall

P. Patterson

From cloud-lets and sky the ea-gles do fly. The King is their lead-er, to help they come nigh. With the beat-ing of their wing, help and suc-cour they bring. The Flow-er Queen's fair daugh-ter the King's son shall win.

2. From moorland and lair the foxes repair.
   The King is their leader, to help they draw near.
   With their tails flaming red, to bring succour they're led.
   The Flower Queen's fair daughter the King's son shall wed.

3. From lake, pool, and stream the fishes' scales gleam.
   The King is their leader, they all serve the Queen.
   With their scales greeny blue they will bring help to you.
   The Flower Queen's fair daughter to the Prince will be true.

THE STORY OF THE QUEEN BEE

C. Comeras   C. Comeras

Thru' the sun - lit mea - dows and
lea - fy glades we sing, _____ As
side by side and mer - ri - ly we
go a - wan - der - ing. _____ Two
clev - er bro - thers sons of a king,
Set out to find what their for - tune would bring.
Tra la la la, Tra la la la,
Tra la la la, la la la la.

THE STORY OF THE QUEEN BEE

C. Comeras   *C. Comeras*

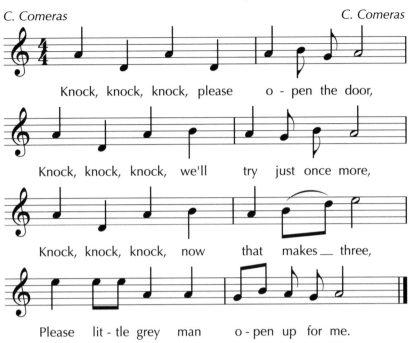

Knock, knock, knock, please   o - pen the door,

Knock, knock, knock, we'll   try   just once more,

Knock, knock, knock,   now   that   makes __ three,

Please   lit - tle grey   man   o - pen up for me.

Recommended Reading

A is for Ox, B. Sanders ISBN 0 679 74285 9 Vintage Books
Failure to Connect, J. Healy ISBN 0 684 85539 9 Simon & Schuster
Set Free Childhood, M. Large. ISBN 1 903458 43 9 Hawthorn Press
Rudolf Steiner - Life, work, inner path and social intentions, R. Lissau
    ISBN 1 869890 06 X Hawthorn Press
Lifeways, G. Davy & B. Voors ISBN 0 950706 24 8 Hawthorn Press
The Spiritual Tasks of the Homemaker, M. Schmidt-Brabant
    ISBN 0 904693 84 8 Temple Lodge Press, England
Education Towards Freedom ISBN 0 906155 32 0 Lanthorn Press, England
Work and Play in Early Childhood, F. Jaffke
    ISBN 0 86315 227 9 Floris Books, Edinburgh, Scotland
Festivals, Family and Food, D. Carey & J. Large
    ISBN 1 950706 23 X Hawthron Press
Festivals Together, S. Fitzjohn, M. Weston & J. Large
    ISBN 1 869890 46 9 Hawthorn Press
Understanding Children's Drawings, M. Strauss
    Rudolf Steiner Press, England
The Wisdom of Fairytales, R. Meyer ISBN 0 86315 208 2 Floris Books
A Guide to Child Health, M. Glöckler & W. Goebel
    ISBN 0 86315 390 9 Floris Books
Education as Preventive Medicine – A Salutogenic Approach,
    M Glöckler ISBN 0 945803 63 X Rudolf Steiner College Press, USA.
Between Form and Freedom, B Staley ISBN 1 869890 08 6 Hawthorn Press
Brothers and Sisters, K. König ISBN 0 86315 446 8 Floris Books
The Challenge of the Will, Margret Meyerkort & Rudi Lissau
    ISBN 0 945803 41 9 Rudolf Steiner College Press, California, USA
The Oxford Nursery Songbook,
    ISBN 0 19 330193 8 Oxford University Press
The Oxford Dictionary of Nursery Rhymes
    ISBN 0 19 860088 7 Oxford University Press